Our
Clothes

Mike Jackson

Illustrated by
John Bennett

Evans

We come from different countries all over the world.

4

We all wear different kinds of clothes.

People all over the world
wear clothes like these.

These boys
live in Peru.

I wear a hat to
shade my face
from the sun.

My hat helps to
keep me warm
in winter, too.

8

Although it's sunny in Peru,
it can be very cold.

9

These girls
come from
Malaysia.

We sometimes wear sarongs.

10

Sarongs feel cool when the weather is hot and damp.

11

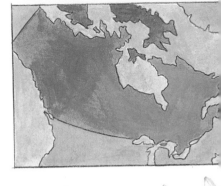

These are
Inuit boys.
They live in Canada.

*I like my thick clothes.
They keep me warm.*

12

In Northern Canada the people wear clothes made from furs.

13

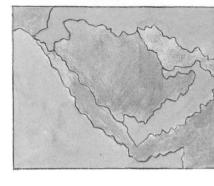

These boys
live in the
Arabian desert.

*My kaffiyeh keeps
the sun and sand
out of my face.*

14

The sun is very hot in the desert and strong winds blow the sand about.

15

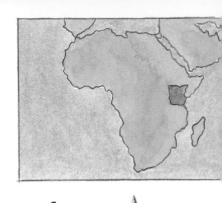

These two children are from Kenya, in Africa.

I like wearing my pretty beads.

The beads are very colourful.

These sisters
live in Japan.

We wear our kimonos
on special occasions.

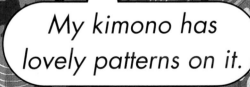

My kimono has
lovely patterns on it.

18

All over the world people have clothes for parties or special occasions.

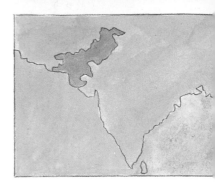

This girl lives in Pakistan.

In many countries people
wear special clothes
for weddings.

21

This girl is from Bali, in Indonesia.

I wear these beautiful clothes for dancing.

Balinese dancing is famous
all over the world.

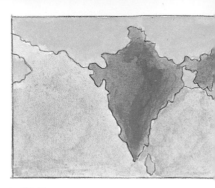

These girls
live in India.

My sari is beautiful.
It is made from silk.

24

Each sari is made from six
metres of silk or cotton.

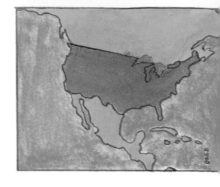

These boys live in North America. They are American Indians.

We like wearing our feathers and buckskins.

26

They wear these clothes for meetings called powwows.

I wear my kimono on special occasions.

I wear warm clothes because it's so cold.

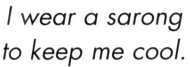

I wear a sarong to keep me cool.

I wear these clothes when I dance.

I wear a kaffiyeh to protect my face.

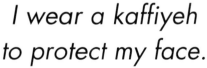

These children come from
different countries all over the
world. Can you remember
where they live?